EXECUTIVE SUMMARY

BACKGROUND

The Office of Inspector (OIG) conducted an audit of Peace Corps/The Gambia (hereafter referred to as "the post") November 12–22, 2013. OIG's fiscal year (FY) 2013 annual plan included the audit, but on August 2, 2013 the post's country director (CD) notified OIG that the post's cashier had failed to properly process a cash deposit until after the missing deposit was discovered by local and headquarters staff. In response to the CD's allegation, OIG announced and conducted the audit. Although the cashier later deposited the funds without a loss occurring, the cashier was terminated for failing to make a timely deposit, as required by Peace Corps policy.

Staff:
- U.S. direct hires: 2
- Foreign service nationals: 1
- Full-time personal services contractors (PSCs): 43

Spending (approx.):
- FY 2013 post spending: $1.6 million
- Average regional overhead: $435,000

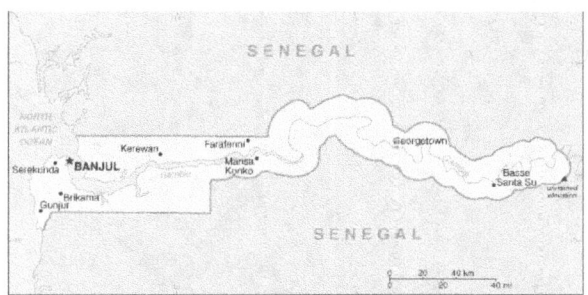
Map of The Gambia

WHAT WE FOUND

The post's financial and administrative operations required improvement in a number of areas and did not fully comply with agency policies and applicable federal laws and regulations. Specifically:

- The director of management and operations (DMO) did not review all of the supporting documents when conducting the monthly cash reconciliation permitting the cashier to retain approximately $1,700 U.S. dollar equivalent (USDE) for 33 days without depositing funds in the U.S. disbursing officer account.

- The post did not properly record and track bills of collection (BOC), permitting the cashier to retain approximately $22,600 USDE outside the imprest fund safe for 79 days without depositing funds in the U.S. disbursing officer account.

- The financial assistant (FA) and the former administrative assistant did not receive sufficient training to effectively perform their duties.

- The agency paid staff medical insurance invoices without complying with requirements for vendor selection and obtaining obligating documents.

- The post did not adequately track and recover payments for employee medical insurance expenses from 2010 to 2013.

We also noted issues with management of medical inventory and adequate separation of duties in management of property and grant projects.

RECOMMENDATIONS IN BRIEF

Our report contains 11 recommendations directed to both the post and headquarters, including: that the post strengthens internal controls over BOCs, review all supporting documents during the monthly cash reconciliation, separate duties for property and grant management, and comply with requirements for vendor selections. We also recommended that the Office of Global Accounts Payable (OGAP) enhance oversight over BOCs.

TABLE OF CONTENTS

BACKGROUND

We conducted this audit of the post November 12–22, 2013. We previously performed a combined audit/program evaluation in August 2003 (IG-03-07-AE). We performed a follow-up audit in October 2005, and issued our report in January 2006 (IG-06-07-FUAE).

Since 1967, more than 1,665 Peace Corps Volunteers have served in The Gambia. At the time of our audit, 74 Volunteers were engaged in the following projects: education, health, and the environment. The post's FY 2013 spending was approximately $1.6 million. In addition, at headquarters, the Africa Region incurred an average of approximately $435,000 per overseas post.[1] Further, in FY 2013, the post received approximately $93,400 from the West Africa Food Security Partnership, a regional partnership between the U.S. Agency for International Development, West African countries, and the Peace Corps, to implement a broad range of activities and interventions at the grassroots level that support the "Feed the Future" program.[2]

Our overall objective in auditing overseas posts is to determine whether the financial and administrative operations are functioning effectively and in compliance with Peace Corps policies and federal regulations during the period under audit. Appendix A provides a full description of our audit objective, scope, and methodology.

AUDIT RESULTS

BILLS OF COLLECTION

The post did not record, track, or monitor BOCs and collections in a timely manner.

The post did not create BOCs in a timely manner, conduct a monthly review of outstanding BOCs, or initiate collection for BOCs relating to vehicle sales and overpayment of staff medical insurance expenses. Peace Corps policy specifies that BOCs are entered as soon as it is known that the Peace Corps will be receiving funds, even if the amount expected is unknown (*Overseas Financial Management Handbook* (OFMH) 7.2.1). Also, a monthly BOC review is required for outstanding BOCs over 30 days (OFMH 7.2.2).[3]

Vehicle Sales. On December 8, 2012, the post sold two vehicles for approximately $22,600 USDE. However, the FA did not create the BOC for 10 days until the cashier received payment

---

[1] The agency was unable to provide the total cost per post as certain costs are centrally budgeted and managed by headquarters offices including the salaries and benefits of U.S. direct hires. The Peace Corps Office of Budget and Analysis provided the total cost incurred by the Africa Region in direct support of its overseas posts, which is an average of $435,000 per post.

[2] Feed the Future, the U.S. government's global hunger and food security initiative, supports country-driven approaches to address the root causes of hunger and poverty. Through this Presidential initiative, the United States is helping countries transform their own agricultural sectors to grow enough food to sustainably feed their people.

[3] The Peace Corps policies and Federal regulations are paraphrased in the report. A complete list of the policies and regulations are listed in Appendix C.

---

confirmation receipts from the buyers. Once the BOC was created, neither the post nor headquarters monitored the collection for the outstanding BOC. At headquarters, OGAP uses the monthly outstanding BOC report to monitor uncollected BOCs and inquire about unusual transactions. However, OGAP did not follow-up about the outstanding BOC because the report excluded BOCs for host country contributions and sale of assets. In January 2013, the funds were not deposited into the bank. The FA noticed large amounts of cash on the floor of the cashier's office that the cashier explained was from the auction sale. The FA instructed the cashier to deposit the funds. Nonetheless, the BOC remained outstanding for 79 days until March 7, 2013, when the cashier deposited the funds and recorded the collection. When post staff does not record BOCs in a timely manner and the monthly BOC reports are not reviewed, the primary controls become ineffective for detecting and preventing misuse of funds.

We also determined that the post lacked sufficient internal controls over imprest funds because the FA failed to ascertain the exact amount of cash on the floor, obtain an explanation for cash being out of the safe, follow up that the deposit was completed, or inform the DMO or cashier liaison about the incident. By not following up on the outstanding collection or informing the DMO of the cash incident, the cashier was not held accountable for adhering to Peace Corps policies relating to cash deposits and was able to retain funds without the post's knowledge.

Employee Medical Insurance Expenses. The local compensation plan and employee contract established a $940 USDE[4] limit per year for health insurance benefits including medical insurance premiums and co-payments for medical treatments received by local staff and their dependents. However, when staff medical expenses exceeded the medical benefit limit, the FA did not consistently invoice staff for the excess expenses.

The post implemented a procedure to track co-payments made to the insurance company in a Microsoft Excel spreadsheet and issued BOCs to staff when payments exceeded the limit. However, we identified 18 instances where the post did not issue BOCs to staff members when the co-payments to the insurance company exceeded the limit. As a result, the agency overpaid staff medical insurance benefits to the post staff.

> **We recommend:**
>
> 1. **That the director of management and operations comply with policy to issue bills of collection as soon as the amount is due to the Peace Corps, even if the exact amount is unknown.**
>
> 2. **That the director of management and operations monitor the outstanding bills of collection log every month and initiate a collection process as required by agency policy.**
>
> 3. **That the director of the Office of Global Accounts Payable modify the monthly bills of collection report to include host country contributions and sale of assets.**

---

[4] The actual local compensation plan limit is 35,000 Dalasis. The limit has been converted into U.S. Dollars using an exchange rate of 1 USD per 37 Dalasis as of November 12, 2013.

4. **That the director of management and operations use the insurance payment tracking spreadsheet to identify staff that exceed the benefits limit and ensure bills of collection are issued to recover these excess payments.**

IMPREST FUNDS

The post did not ensure that the cashier physically deposited funds in a timely manner.

According to the *Cashier's User Guide*

> The cashier is never authorized to process a deposit in the cashier software to reduce accountability and hold the funds in the cashier safe. Deposits entered into an ACP [automated cashiering program] must only occur on a day when a physical deposit will be made...The cashier supervisor is responsible for ensuring that physical deposits are made in conjunction with deposits entered into the cashier program.

The post collected $2,132 USDE from property sold during the May 11, 2013, auction. The FA issued a BOC for the sale of the property on May 17, 2013, but the cashier did not issue the cash receipt until June 18, 2013, which was 38 days after the funds were collected. On June 26, 2013, the cashier entered a deposit for $1,711 USDE into the post's financial reporting system, but the cashier did not physically deposit the funds until July 29, 2013 (33 days later). On June 27, 2013, the day after the cashier entered the deposit the DMO conducted a reconciliation of the imprest fund but did not review all of the supporting documents.

The DMO failed to review the supporting documents during the cash reconciliation, and as a result, the cashier was able to retain funds without the post realizing the funds were missing. The administrative assistant noticed that the bank deposit slip was missing and contacted the cashier for the missing document, but the cashier did not give the administrative assistant the document. Despite not having the bank deposit slip, the post mailed the remaining supporting documents to headquarters. Once the documents were received, headquarters' staff noticed the bank deposit slip was missing. Headquarters' staff was able to obtain confirmation from the bank that the cashier did not deposit the funds until July 29, 2013. As a result, the cashier was terminated from the Peace Corps for not timely depositing funds as required by Peace Corps policy.

We recommend:

5. **That the director of management and operations review all of the supporting documents when conducting the monthly unannounced cash reconciliation and ensure that bank deposits slips are included for deposits.**

The post did not fully comply with requirements for vendor selection.

Despite Peace Corps policy, the post did not obtain written quotes, retain proof of advertising, prepare selection memos, or complete a justification memo to document the selection of medical staff insurance and leasehold improvements. According to policy, for procurements expected to exceed $10,000 the contracting officer shall solicit the contract and obtain written competitive quotes from at least three qualified suppliers. Justification memos are required when there is lack of adequate documentation *(Peace Corps Manual* section 732.6). Policy further states that individual purchases are not allowed to be separated for the purpose of using the small purchase method *(Federal Acquisition Regulation* section 13.003(c)(2). In addition, policy states that purchases greater than $25,000 will need a copy of the proposed contract, selection memo, country director clearance form, quotes and purchase request package *(Peace Corps Contracting Handbook).*

Medical Staff Insurance. The post provided local staff medical insurance per the local compensation plan approved by the U.S. Embassy. PSC contracts authorize commitments of medical insurance payments but the post did not solicit bids for the insurance contracts from 2010–13, obtain written quotes from vendors, prepare selection or justification memos, or include the contracting officer in the selection process. Instead, the post relied on the staff committee to annually select the vendors, verbally notified the DMO of the vendor selection, and then the contracting officer procured the services. From 2010 to 2013, the post disbursed approximately $171,000 USDE for medical expenses. Without proper competition, it is difficult to ascertain if the agency received a reasonable price for the medical services rendered.

Leasehold Improvements. In FY 2012, the post contracted with the property owner to perform leasehold improvements to the main office building. The property owner increased two separate invoices by $20,000 USDE for the building modifications totaling $40,000 USDE. However, the post did not solicit bids or document the justification for selecting the property owner to perform the improvements as required by Peace Corps policy. Requiring written solicitations helps ensure fair contracting practices and the most economical acquisitions.

> **We recommend:**
>
> 6. **That the director of management and operations follow policy and obtain written competitive bids for purchases that exceed $10,000.**

DISBURSEMENTS

The agency paid approximately $137,000 USDE of local staff medical insurance invoices without signing contracts.

Section 32.8.1 of OFMH states that all post obligations need to be printed and signed obligation documents such as a contract or grant form. Contrary to Peace Corps policy, the agency did not have valid obligating documents to support the staff medical payments to medical insurance vendors since the contracting officer did not sign the medical insurance contracts for 2011 through 2013. In 2011, the post used the same insurance company from 2010 without obtaining a contract extension. For 2012 and 2013, the post selected different insurance carriers with new contracts signed by the vendors. However, the post's contracting officer did not sign either of the contracts. Without signed contracts from the contracting officer, it is difficult to ensure that the contract actions were completed by the contracting officer and that the terms were agreed upon.

The post did not properly record leasehold improvements as capital assets.

The post disbursed $40,000 to the landlord to perform leasehold improvements on the first and second floor of the main office building. However, the agency did not record the $40,000 USDE leasehold improvements as capital assets. As a result, the agency's financial records were misstated and the costs of the improvement were not depreciated in accordance with accounting standards.

According to the *Federal Accounting Standard Advisory Board's Statement on Federal Financial Accounting Standards 6*, "Accounting for Property, Plant, and Equipment," "Costs which either extend the useful life of existing general PP&E, or enlarge or improve its capacity shall be capitalized and depreciated/amortized over the remaining useful life of the associated general PP&E."

We recommend:

7. **That the director of management and operations enter into a contract with the insurance company, signed by both parties including the contracting officer, to serve as the obligating document.**

8. **That the post properly record leasehold improvements as a capital asset in accordance with the Statement on Federal Financial Accounting Standards, Accounting for Property, Plant and Equipment.**

PROPERTY

The post did not properly separate duties over property management.

According to the Government Accountability Office (GAO)'s report on standards for internal control in the federal government, "Key duties and responsibilities are divided among different people to reduce the risk of error, waste or fraud (GAO's *Internal Control Management and Evaluation Tool)*. In addition, Peace Corps policy specifies that property management duties for purchasing an item, entering it into the database and conducting inventory should be separated. The same person maintaining the database should not be conducting the annual inventory (*Personal Property Management Handbook*).

Despite Peace Corps policy, the DMO assigned the property manager to record property into BarTracks, the post's property management system, and conduct the annual physical count. By maintaining the official property records and conducting the annual count, the property manager had the ability to remove an item from the records and cover up the loss by scanning the detached bar code. Although we did not identify any improper actions, this concentration of duties is contrary to the agency's policy and exposed the agency to unnecessary risks.

> **We recommend:**
>
> 9. **That the director of management and operations follow agency guidance and separate the responsibilities of BarTracks database maintenance from conducting inventories.**

GRANTS

The post did not establish adequate separation of duties in managing the grant process and crucial information was missing from the grant tracking worksheet.

GAO's report on internal control standards for the federal government state "key duties are divided among different people." Also, "no one individual is allowed to control all aspects of a transaction or event (Government Accountability Office (GAO)'s *Internal Control Management and Evaluation Tool)*. In addition, Peace Corps policy specifies that the billing function is separate from the cash collection (OFMH 7.1).

Contrary to the internal control standards, the post did not separate grants management from the review process and the billing function from cash collection. The grant coordinator performed several duties including coordinating the selection of grants, tracking the status, monitoring the projects and reconciling the completion report with the supporting documents. For any amount due, the grants coordinator collected the funds from the Volunteer and provided cash and the completion report to the FA for safe keeping and issuing a BOC. Although we did not identify any improper actions, the concentration of duties in one staff member was not in keeping with GAO principles of internal control and exposed the agency to unnecessary risks.

While reviewing the grant management process, we also noted that the grant tracking worksheet did not include the Volunteer's close of service date or the project's expected completion date. Without this information, it is difficult for the grant coordinator to follow-up with Volunteers in a timely manner to remind them to submit the completion reports and support prior to their close of service.

> **We recommend:**
>
> 10. **That the director of management and operations reassign duties for reviewing the completion report and supporting documentation to an administrative staff member, and cash collection to only the cashier.**

11. **That the director of management and operations add the Volunteer's close of service date or the project's expected completion date in the grant tracking sheets.**

OTHER AREAS OF CONCERN

We noted the following additional areas that could be improved to enhance efficiency.

The FA and the former administrative assistant (AA) did not receive adequate training to effectively perform their duties.

The FA and the former administrative assistant did not receive adequate training to effectively perform their duties. The FA did not comply with Peace Corps policy to issue BOCs before cash collection and follow up on outstanding BOCs. According to the FA, the agency did not provide any training on Peace Corps policies and procedures for the position. The FA was unaware of the policies outlined in the *Peace Corps Manual* and the *Overseas Financial Management Handbook*.

The AA also did not comply with Peace Corps policy on creating BOCs when the debt was known because the AA thought that the process created unnecessary paperwork and was a waste of time. The AA explained that if the post issued BOCs prior to determining the final amount, it was highly likely that the BOC amount would be incorrect. This would require the AA to void it before creating another BOC in the correct amount. Nonetheless, creating a BOC when the debt is known is an internal control procedure that is used to safeguard assets, maintain accurate records and establish a system of checks and balances.

We did not issue a recommendation to the post for providing adequate staff training as this matter has been referred to Office of Inspector General's Evaluation Unit for consideration in its evaluation of Peace Corps' Overseas Staff Training Programs.

The post's medical supply inventory was not current or complete.

The post's medical supply inventory system did not have accurate amounts for five medical supplies classified as either specially designated or controlled substances because the medical unit did not update the medical supply inventory control clerk when the amounts changed. During the physical verification of medical supplies we noted four instances where the physical inventory count for specially designated supplies did not match the medical inventory tracking sheet. In addition, a controlled substance included in the narcotics log was not recorded. The Office of Health Services explained that all controlled drugs should be recorded in the medical inventory system. Without an accurate medical inventory system, the post increases the risk of theft or misuse of medical supplies.

We have noted similar errors in the physical count at several other posts we have recently audited and issued a recommendation. We noted this issue in *Capstone Report: 2012 Medical Inventory Issues* (August 2013). Accordingly, we are not issuing a separate recommendation in this report.

The post did not comply with Peace Corps policies and procedures for disposal of supplies.

The post did not dispose of medical supplies on a quarterly basis. According to the Office of Health Services, the post could dispose of medical supplies every six months if the post did not have large quantities of expired medical supplies. During our review of the FY 2010 to FY 2013 disposal authorization forms for medical inventory items, we noted numerous instances where the medical supplies were disposed of several months after the expiration date; in some instances after two years. Per the CD, the delay in disposal was the result of the post receiving expired supplies from a closed Peace Corps post. By not timely disposing of expired medical supplies, post increases the chance of dispensing expired medication to Volunteers.

We also noted that the CD and the Peace Corps Medical Officer inappropriately flushed down the toilet expired medical supplies. The disposal authorization forms indicated flushing as the method for medical supply disposal. Although there is no indication of environmental effects due to flushing, U.S. government environmental agencies oppose adding drug residue into water systems. The post has since built an incinerator to dispose of expired medical supplies and will use Medical Research Council lab for exceptional cases.

We did not issue a recommendation to the post regarding medical disposal because we noted improper disposal of medical supplies at several other posts we have recently audited and deem it to be a systemic issue. See *Capstone Report: 2012 Medical Inventory Issues* (August 2013).

The CD did not comply with vendor selection requirements when contracting pre-service training (PST) facilities.

The post used the same training facility for approximately 20 years. The CD signed the most recent contract in 2009 for $20,860. We were unable to determine if the post followed the acquisition procedures outlined in MS 732 because the post lacked documentation or justification as to why this contract was executed. Specifically, there was no notice of solicitation, documentation of the bids reviewed, or justification for the selection. Furthermore, we did not find any documentation supporting that the post made a price reasonableness determination for the procurement.

We have noted similar procurement practices prior to 2011 at other posts that were non – compliant with applicable federal and Peace Corps guidance. We noted these issues in the *Final Audit Report: Peace Corps' Process for Soliciting, Awarding, and Administering Contracts* (August 2010). Since the 2010 audit, the Office of Acquisitions and Contract Management have reduced the CD's procurement authority from $100,000 to $3,000. Accordingly, we are not questioning the PST costs in this report.

The post did not implement safeguards to secure the imprest funds.

The Cashier User Guide states:

> Combinations on the cashier safe are required to be changed; (I). At least once a year: The combination should always be changed and set by the cashier. (II). When there is a change in cashiers: An outgoing cashier should not turn over the combination to an incoming cashier. (III). When the combination has been compromised: This can include times when cashier fraud is suspected or has been detected, when post management has had to open the safe in an emergency situation (cashier is absent), when it is suspected that the combination has been disclosed.

In July 2013, the post hired a new cashier to manage the imprest funds but due to mechanical issues, the cashier's safe would not open. Since the cashier's safe would not open, the cashier used the alternate cashier's safe (located in the cashier's cage) and the alternate cashier's safe combination to operate the imprest fund. Contrary to Peace Corps policy, the new cashier did not change the safe combination before using it. The post's failure to change the combination to the cashier's safe jeopardized the safety of the imprest funds.

While post management was aware that the safe combination had to be changed, it needed technical assistance to change it. The post contacted the U.S. Embassy's regional security officer (RSO) to assist it with changing the safe combination; however this duty is not the responsibility of the RSO. The safe combination was not changed until a new safe, which was ordered prior to the audit, arrived in February 2014.

We did not issue a recommendation for post to change the safe combination because the post received a new safe after the audit, and the cashier changed the combination and provided the new combination to the embassy's RSO. Furthermore, the post has implemented a logging system to track when the combination changed and the person who changed it.

QUESTIONED COSTS AND
FUNDS TO BE PUT TO BETTER USE

We did not identify funds to be put to better use. We identified the following unsupported costs (a category of questioned costs) during the course of the audit.

Recommendation number	Description	Amount
6	Staff Medical Insurance	$171,000
6	Leasehold Improvements	$40,000

The Inspector General Act of 1978, as amended, defines funds to be put to better use and questioned costs

- "Funds to be put to better use" are funds that could be used more efficiently if management took actions to implement and complete the recommendation.

- "Questioned costs" are costs that are questioned because of an alleged violation of a provision of a law, regulation, contract, grant, cooperative agreement or document governing expenditure of funds; a finding that, at the time of the audit, such cost is not supported by adequate documentation; or a finding that the expenditure of funds for the intended purpose is unnecessary or unreasonable.

LIST OF RECOMMENDATIONS

We recommend:

1. That the director of management and operations comply with policy to issue bills of collection as soon as the amount is due to the Peace Corps, even if the exact amount is unknown.

2. That the director of management and operations monitor the outstanding bills of collection log every month and initiate a collection process as required by agency policy.

3. That the director of the Office of Global Accounts Payable modify the monthly bills of collection report to include host country contributions and sale of assets.

4. That the director of management and operations use the insurance payment tracking spreadsheet to identify staff that exceed the benefits limit and ensure bills of collection are issued to recover these excess payments.

5. That the director of management and operations review all of the supporting documents when conducting the monthly unannounced cash reconciliation and ensure that bank deposits slips are included for deposits.

6. That the director of management and operations follow policy and obtain written competitive bids for purchases that exceed $10,000.

7. That the director of management and operations enter into a contract with the insurance company, signed by both parties including the contracting officer, to serve as the obligating document.

8. That post properly record leasehold improvements as a capital asset in accordance with the Statement on Federal Financial Accounting Standards, Accounting for Property, Plant and Equipment.

9. That the director of management and operations follow agency guidance and separate the responsibilities of BarTracks database maintenance from conducting inventories.

10. That the director of management and operations reassign duties for reviewing the completion report and supporting documentation to an administrative staff member, and cash collection to only the cashier.

11. That the director of management and operations add the Volunteer's close of service date or the project's expected completion date in the grant tracking sheets.

APPENDIX A: OBJECTIVE, SCOPE, AND METHODOLOGY

Our objective in auditing overseas posts is to determine whether the financial and administrative operations are functioning effectively and comply with Peace Corps policies and federal regulations. Our audit conclusions are based on information from three sources: (1) document and data analysis, (2) interviews, and (3) direct observation. We conducted this performance audit in accordance with *Generally Accepted Government Auditing Standards*. Those standards require that we plan and perform the audit to obtain sufficient, appropriate evidence to provide a reasonable basis for our findings and conclusions based on our audit objectives. We believe that the evidence obtained provides a reasonable basis for our findings and conclusions based on our audit objectives.

The audit covered fiscal years 2010, 2011, 2012, and 2013. While at the post, we interviewed key staff including the CD, DMO, staff responsible for administrative support, and the lead Peace Corps medical officer. We communicated issues and areas of improvement to senior staff at post and Peace Corps management at headquarters and included significant issues noted during our audit in this report. We primarily reviewed the following processes and associated controls:

- BOCs
- Contracts and leases
- Cash and Non-cash payments
- Imprest fund
- Credit card transactions
- Information technology general controls
- Medical supplies
- Personal property and vehicles
- Personal services contracts
- Volunteer payments

Although we could not independently verify the reliability of all this information, we compared it with other available supporting documents to determine data consistency and reasonableness. We relied on the results of the annual Federal Information Security Management Act review, which did not identify deficiencies with data reliability that would impact our audit. Based on these efforts, we believe the information we obtained is sufficiently reliable for this report.

Our audit criteria were derived from the following sources: Financial Accounting Standards Advisory Board's Statement on Federal Accounting Standards, the *Peace Corps Manual, the Overseas Financial Management Handbook, Peace Corps Overseas Contracting Handbook, Peace Corps Personal Property Management Handbook,* and other Peace Corps policies and initiatives. Throughout the audit, auditors were aware of the possibility or existence of fraud, waste, or misuse significant to the audit objectives and conducted procedures designed to obtain reasonable assurance of detecting any such fraud as deemed appropriate.

AA	Administrative Assistant
BOC	Bill of Collection
CD	Country Director
DMO	Director of Management and Operations
FA	Financial Assistant
FY	Fiscal Year
GAO	Government Accountability Office
PST	Pre-Service Training
OFMH	Overseas Financial Management Handbook
OGAP	Office of Global Accounts Payable
OIG	Office of Inspector General
PSC	Personal Services Contractor
RSO	Regional Security Officer
USDE	United States Dollar Equivalent

APPENDIX C: CRITERIA USED TO SUPPORT ISSUES IN THE REPORT

Federal Requirements

FEDERAL ACQUSITION REGULATION

The *Federal Acquisition Regulation* (FAR) *13.003 (c) (2),* "Simplified Acquisition Procedure" states

> (c) (2) Do not break down requirements aggregating more than the simplified acquisition threshold (or for commercial items, the threshold in Subpart 13.5) or the micro-purchase threshold into several purchases that are less than the applicable threshold merely to—
> (1) Permit use of simplified acquisition procedures; or
> (2) Avoid any requirement that applies to purchases exceeding the micro-purchase threshold.

THE FEDERAL ACCOUNTING STANDARD ADVISORY BOARD STATEMENT ON FEDERAL FINANCIAL ACCOUNTING STANDARDS

The Federal Accounting Standard Advisory Board's Statement on Federal Financial Accounting Standards 6, "Accounting for Property, Plant, and Equipment (PP&E)" states

> PP&E is defined as tangible assets that (1) have an estimated useful life of 2 or more years, (2) are not intended for sale in the ordinary course of business, and (3) are intended to be used or available for use by the entity…Costs which either extend the useful life of existing general PP&E, or enlarge or improve its capacity shall be capitalized and depreciated/amortized over the remaining useful life of the associated general PP&E.

Peace Corps Requirements

CASHIER USER GUIDE

The *Cashier's User Guide* states

> The cashier is never authorized to process a deposit in the cashier software to reduce accountability and hold the funds in the cashier safe. Deposits entered into an ACP (automated cashiering program) must only occur on a day when a physical deposit will be made…The cashier supervisor is responsible for ensuring that physical deposits are made in conjunction with deposits entered into the cashier program.

OVERSEAS FINANCIAL MANAGEMENT HANDBOOK

The Overseas Financial Management Handbook states

> The Billing Officer performs the following tasks as soon as the debt is known, even if the exact amount isn't known*: For internal control reasons, BOCs are entered as soon as it is known that Peace Corps will be receiving funds, even if the exact amount is not known (for example, HCC or VAT). It is very important that this Bill be entered in FOR Post at the moment it is identified (see 7.2.1).

"Obligating Documents to File at the Post" states in part, "All Post obligations need printed and signed obligating documents." If a form other than the FOR Post PC-2060 is the obligating document (for example, TA, contract, grant form), that form should be signed and filed (see 32.8.1).

PEACE CORPS MANUAL

The *Peace Corps Manual* 732, 6.3.6, "Overseas Purchases - Purchases for More Than 10% of the Small Purchase Limitation Threshold" states

> When the expected purchase price exceeds 10% of the small purchase limitation threshold, the Contracting Officer shall solicit at least three bids from qualified suppliers, if available… Written quotations shall be required (except for emergency supplies and perishable substances) when the estimated dollar amount of the purchase exceeds $10,000.00.

> For proposed contract actions expected to exceed $10,000.00, Contracting Officers shall disseminate information by posting the notice of solicitation or a copy of the solicitation in a public place at the Peace Corps Office for a least 10 days prior to the closing date for receipt of solicitations or bids. Contracting Officers shall place paid advertisements of proposed contracts when it is anticipated that effective competition cannot be obtained otherwise….
> The determination that a proposed price is reasonable should be based on competitive quotations. If only one response is received, or the price variance between multiple responses reflects lack of adequate competition, a statement shall be included in the contract file giving the basis of the determination of fair and reasonable price.

PEACE CORPS OVERSEAS CONTRACTING HANDBOOK

The Peace Corps' *Overseas Contracting Handbook* states, "For all overseas procurements, both services and supplies, greater than $25,000 the following is needed: a copy of proposed contract, appropriate selection memo, country director clearance form, copy of the request for quotes and copy of the purchase request package."

PEACE CORPS PROPERTY MANAGEMENT HANDBOOK

The Peace Corps' *Property Management Handbook* states, "Duties must be assigned to separate people. If the same person is purchasing an item, entering it into the database and inventorying it, there are increased chances of both mistakes and actual fraud."

Other Guidance

The Government Accountability Office *Internal Control Management and Evaluation Tool* states

> Key duties and responsibilities are divided or segregated among different people to reduce the risk of error, waste, or fraud.

> • No one individual is allowed to control all key aspects of a transaction or event.
> • Responsibilities and duties involving transactions and events are separated among different employees with respect to authorization, approval, processing and recording, making payments or receiving funds, review and auditing, and the custodial functions and handling of related assets.
> • Duties are assigned systematically to a number of individuals to ensure that effective checks and balances exist.

• Where feasible, no one individual is allowed to work alone with cash, negotiable securities, or other highly venerable asset.

APPENDIX D: AGENCY'S RESPONSE TO THE PRELIMINARY REPORT

MEMORANDUM

To:	Kathy Buller, Inspector General
Through:	Daljit K. Bains, Chief Compliance Officer
From:	Dick Day, Regional Director for Africa Jennifer Goette, Country Director
Date:	August 15, 2014
CC:	Carrie Hessler-Radelet, Director Laura Chambers, Chief of Staff Joaquin Ferrao, Deputy Inspector General Snehal Nanavati, Lead Auditor Carolos Torres, Associate Director, Global Operations Carl Swartz, Africa Region Chief of Operations Nicole Shire, Director of Management Operations, PC/The Gambia Greg Kennedy, Programming and Training Manager, PC/The Gambia Zachary Rosen, Country Desk Officer Patricia Barkle, Deputy Chief Compliance Officer
Subject:	Agency Response to the Preliminary Report of Peace Corps/The Gambia Project No. 13-AUD-08, June 2014

Enclosed please find the agency's response to the recommendations made by the Inspector General for Peace Corps/The Gambia outlined in the Preliminary Report sent to the Agency on June 11, 2014.

The Region concurs with 11 recommendations provided by the OIG in its Preliminary Audit Report: Peace Corps/The Gambia Project No. 13-AUD-08. Post has addressed and provided supporting documentation for 6 of the 11 recommendations and will work to address the remaining recommendations by the set target dates.

The Region will continue to work with Post and the departments identified in the Preliminary Report to ensure closure of these recommendations by the dates included within for outstanding recommendations.

Recommendation 1

That the Director of Management and Operations comply with policy to issue bills of collection as soon as the amount is due to the Peace Corps, even if the exact amount is unknown.

Concur :

Response:

The agency policy regarding the issuing of bills of collection was shared with Africa Region directors of management and operations at their conference in July 2013. This was presented during Paul Shea's sessions on Cashiering. DMOs were informed that if there was any known debt that their post was going to have to collect on that they should establish a bill of collection in advance of an invoice being issued by a vendor. As of July 2013, Post has been issuing bills of collection for any known debt and they will continue to do so.

Documents Submitted:
- 365 and 99 reports from FOR Post that show how long Bills of Collection have been outstanding and when they are collected. It can show the date a BOC was established and when it was collected for known debts.

Documents to be Submitted:

Status and Timeline for Completion:
Completed

Recommendation 2

That the Director of Management and Operations monitor the outstanding bills of collection log every month and initiate a collection process as required by agency policy.

Concur:

Response:
Following the visit from the OIG, as part of Post's new standard operating procedures, Peace Corps/The Gambia has decided that the DMO will review the bill of collection after every monthly cash count. The DMO currently does review the bill of collection log after every monthly cash count. In reviewing the 365-99 reports the DMO ensures that there are no outstanding bills of collection for more than one month and the DMO will follow up with anyone who hasn't reconciled their bill of collection.

Documents Submitted:

Documents to be Submitted:
- Standard operating procedure related to bills of collection
- 99 Report

Status and Timeline for Completion:
September 15, 2014

Recommendation 3

That the Director of the Office of Global Accounts Payable modify the monthly bills of collection report to include host country contributions and sale of assets.

Concur

Response:

The Director of the Office of Global Accounts Payable has worked with the FOR Post support team to modify the monthly bill of collection report to include the host country contributions and sale of assets.

Documents Submitted:
Copy of most recent bill of collection report

Documents to be Submitted:

Status and Timeline for Completion:
Completed

Recommendation 4

That the Director of Management and Operations use the insurance payment tracking spreadsheet to identify staff that exceed the benefits limit and ensure bills of collection are issued to recover these excess payments.

Concur:

Response:
Obligations for staff insurance are now created for individual staff members for the full amount. It is impossible for staff to exceed their medical insurance allowance. Invoices are issued from the insurance company to the staff member once they have exceeded their allowance.

Documents Submitted:
Insurance tracking sheet

Examples of obligations from FOR Post
Status of Obligation Report

Documents to be Submitted:

Status and Timeline for Completion:
Completed

Recommendation 5

That the Director of Management and Operations review all of the supporting documents when conducting the monthly unannounced cash reconciliation and ensure that bank deposits slips are included for deposits.

Concur:

Response:

Post recognizes that collection done by cashiers is not the final step in the process and that in Post's new bill of collection standard operating procedures they have clearly delineated the steps that need to be taken by the DMO to verify that the cashier has completed all necessary steps in making a deposit to the USDO account. By looking at deposit slips, the DMO will verify that the deposit has been made. This verification will be done during the monthly unannounced cash count.

Documents Submitted:

Documents to be Submitted:
- Sample bank deposit slip
- Standard operating procedure related to bills of collection,

Status and Timeline for Completion:
September 15, 2014

Recommendation 6

That the Director of Management and Operations follow policy and obtain written competitive bids for purchases that exceed $10,000.

Concur:

Response:
Post in effect, did not always carefully document the competition that was done in receiving competitive bids for purchases over $10,000. The process was happening, but not completed with adding the necessary proof to the procurement file. Post is carefully monitoring OFMH section 44 and MS 732 6.3 which clearly outlines how procurement must be done. Post will also ensure all procurement files have documentation to prove

that competitive bidding occurred during the procurement process. Since 2012 Post has been collecting competitive bids and placing them in the relevant procurement files for specific vendors where purchases exceeded $10,000.

<u>Documents Submitted</u>:
- Example of a recent Selection memo for purchases over $10,000
- Examples of three quotes solicited
- Example of obligating and liquidation documents for the purchase

<u>Documents to be Submitted:</u>

<u>Status and Timeline for Completion:</u>
Completed

<u>Recommendation 7</u>

That the Director of Management and Operations enter into a contract with the insurance company, signed by both parties including the contracting officer, to serve as the obligating document.

<u>Concur:</u>

<u>Response:</u>

Following the visit from the IG, Post realizes that even though committees were formed to analyze different insurance companies year over year, there was an expectation that a full contract be written up with the insurance company on an annual basis and that documentation will be put into the files to prove that there was a competitive process for choosing the company. Moving forward, Post will make sure that they properly document the contract file with the insurance company to prove that a competitive process was put in place and that a contract was drafted which meets Peace Corps standards to provide health insurance to employees. This was done for FY14. Post would like to note that for previous years, valid obligating documents were in place and an agreement negotiated with a company was reached, though Post was unaware that this was considered a contractual agreement since this was for a service of health insurance throughout a year according to the local compensation plan.

<u>Documents Submitted:</u>
- FY14 Insurance contract

<u>Documents to be Submitted:</u>

<u>Status and Timeline for Completion:</u>
Completed

Recommendation 8

That the post properly record leasehold improvements as a capital asset in accordance with the Statement on Federal Financial Accounting Standards, Accounting for Property, Plant and Equipment.

Concur:

Response:

The agency is making a better effort to ensure posts properly account for capital assets according to the plan for property, plant and equipment. When leasehold improvements are done moving forward, they will be properly allocated to the relevant budget line dedicated to them. Post has not had any leasehold improvement since 2012 so we are including the memo to document the current understanding.

Documents Submitted:

Documents to be Submitted:
- Memo standard operating procedure to staff

Status and Timeline for Completion:
October 31, 2014

Recommendation 9

That the Director of Management and Operations follow agency guidance and separate the responsibilities of BarTracks database maintenance from conducting inventories.

Concur:

Response:

Following the audit and this recommendation Post has now given separate responsibility to staff members that are receiving property from those that are updating the BarTracks inventory systems. The Post IT Specialist receives property, the Property Manager does inventory and the General Services Assistant does the scanning. Those divisions will be stated in a standard operating procedure and will be included in a each individual's scope of work. This is in compliance with agency guidance which states that there must be separate responsibilities of BarTracks database maintenance and conducting inventories.

Documents Submitted:

Documents to be Submitted:
- Standard operating procedure related to BarTracks

- Revised SOW for staff involved in the inventory process

Status and Timeline for Completion:
October 1, 2014

Recommendation 10

That the Director of Management and Operations reassign duties for reviewing the completion report and supporting documentation to an administrative staff member, and cash collection to only the cashier.

Concur:

Response:
Duties have been reassigned. DMO reviews the completion report and supporting documentation and cash is only collected by the cashier. There is a clear separation of duties and a standard operating procedure will establish the policy.

Documents Submitted:

Documents to be Submitted:
- Standard operating procedure related to the completion report.

Status and Timeline for Completion:
September 15, 2014

Recommendation 11

That the Director of Management and Operations add the Volunteer's close of service date or the project's expected completion date in the grant tracking sheets.

Concur:

Response:

While the IG was at post, Post added columns for a Volunteer's close of service date along with the project's expected completion date to the grants tracking sheet. In addition, as part of the Close of Service process, Post verifies that all grants have been completed or reassigned.

Documents Submitted:
- Grants tracking sheet

Documents to be Submitted:

Status and Timeline for Completion:
Completed

APPENDIX E: OIG COMMENTS

Management concurred with all 11 recommendations. All 11 recommendations will remain open pending confirmation from the chief compliance officer that the documentation identified in management's response has been received. In its response, management described actions it is taking, or intends to take, to address the issues that prompted each of our recommendations.

We wish to note that in closing recommendations, we are not certifying that the region or post has taken these actions, nor that we have reviewed their effect. Certifying compliance and verifying effectiveness are management's responsibilities. However, when we feel it is warranted, we may conduct a follow-up review to confirm that action has been taken and to evaluate the impact.

APPENDIX F: AUDIT COMPLETION AND OIG CONTACT

AUDIT COMPLETION

This audit was conducted under the direction of Acting Assistant Inspector General for Audit Hal Nanavati and Auditor Renita Davis.

Judy Leonhardt

Judy Leonhardt
Assistant Inspector General for Audit

OIG CONTACT

If you wish to comment on the quality or usefulness of this report to help us strengthen our product, please contact Acting Assistant Inspector General for Audit Hal Nanavati at snanavati@peacecorps.gov or 202.692.2929.